How...
Mystery
Shopper 101

How to Start, Grow, and Succeed in Mystery Shopping From A to Z

HowExpert with Penny Hodgin

Copyright HowExpert™
www.HowExpert.com

For more tips related to this topic, visit HowExpert.com/mysteryshopper.

Recommended Resources

- HowExpert.com – Quick 'How To' Guides on All Topics by Everyday Experts.
- HowExpert.com/books – HowExpert Books
- HowExpert.com/products – HowExpert Products
- HowExpert.com/courses – HowExpert Courses
- HowExpert.com/clothing – HowExpert Clothing
- HowExpert.com/membership – Learn All Topics from A to Z by Real Experts.
- HowExpert.com/affiliates – HowExpert Affiliate Program
- HowExpert.com/jobs – HowExpert Jobs
- HowExpert.com/writers – Write About Your #1 Passion/Knowledge/Expertise.
- YouTube.com/HowExpert – Subscribe to HowExpert YouTube.
- Instagram.com/HowExpert – Follow HowExpert on Instagram.
- Facebook.com/HowExpert – Follow HowExpert on Facebook.

Table of Contents

Chapter 1: Mystery Shopping: What It Is and What It's Not

Types of Work

What do you envision when you think of the average day in the life of a mystery shopper? Do you see you and your friends enjoying a day out at the mall, laughing with bags of free merch in tow? Or maybe you and your partner lounging poolside at a 5-star luxury beach resort? How about you cruising down a scenic highway while test driving a high-end roadster? All of these scenarios are a possibility for mystery shoppers!

When you first start out mystery shopping your day will probably look more like you picking up some dinner in the drive-thru of a local fast food place or stopping by department store to inquire about a new appliance. It may not be as glamorous as you first thought but it makes up for it in flexibility and variety. You're guaranteed to have an ever-changing list of tasks and scenarios to complete with literally hundreds of different companies that provide mystery shopping services to clients. Those clients can be anything from mass merchants to specialty stores to financial institutions to car dealerships & beyond!

The jobs you will complete, known as shops in the mystery shopping industry, for these companies can be categorized as covert or revealed and in-person or remote.

Covert vs. Revealed Shops

Covert shops are shops in which you do not reveal yourself as a mystery shopper to anyone. This means you will make contact with a business location in person or via phone/web, complete your assigned scenario, make required observations as provided in your shop instructions, and report your observations back to the mystery shopping company. At no point during a covert shop should you reveal to store employees, management, or customers that you are anything other than a typical customer. Covert shops are by far the most common type of mystery shop...in fact, they are what puts the "mystery" in mystery shop!

Covert shops may also require you to assume an alternate identity. You may be required to give the employee at the shop location a fake name, fake job or financial information, fake address, etc. You will always be provided the exact details of the shop scenario, including any fake information you need to provide, in the shop's instructions. These shops would obviously require more extensive preparation beforehand to familiarize yourself with your new identity. For example, I have completed shops at financial institutions where I was required to portray a person with a high income and various investments. All of the fake information I had to provide (i.e. salary, investment amounts, etc.) was spelled out in the shop's instructions, which were provided to me well in advance of the shop's assigned completion date. This way I was able to plan out and practice the scenario ahead of time so that my answers sounded as natural as possible during the shop.

Video mystery shopping is probably the fastest growing segment of the mystery shopping industry. In fact, some companies specialize in video shopping, such as The Shadow Agency (https://shadowagency.shopmetrics.com/login.asp). Video shopping is the ultimate covert shopping, because the end client is able to see and hear the interaction exactly as it happened, taking the burden of extensive explanation off of the shopper. Shoppers are often required to purchase their own video equipment prior to completing video shops, while some companies will provide equipment. The PV500 camera is the most popular choice for video shops. As video shops are expected to become even more popular in the future, if you find that you enjoy traditional non-video mystery shops, you may want to consider investing in the equipment and training necessary for video shops.

Revealed shops require you to reveal your status as a mystery shopper to the store management or employees at some point during the shop. This would typically be done at the end of the shop after playing out the assigned scenario and making the required observations. When revealing your identity to store management or employees you will be provided a script to use by the mystery shopping company in your shop's instructions.

Revealed shops sometimes involve some type of on-the-spot reward for the employee or location being shopped, such as a gift card. While it can be exciting to give an employee a reward for a successful shop it can also be very stressful to have to inform an employee that they did not complete the requirements in order to receive the reward. It is important for you to be aware of the possibility of having to deliver bad news to an employee and avoid these types of shops if you do not have the temperament to deal with the stress that this can bring along. While it is rare, employees can sometimes react poorly to receiving news that their shop was unsuccessful. Maintaining professionalism is a must in these situations.

In-person vs. Remote Shops

In-person shops are shops where you visit a physical business location to conduct the mystery shop. These shops almost always involve interacting with an employee. You will gather identifying information (i.e. age, height, hair color, gender, clothing, etc.) about the employees you interact with, time certain parts of the interactions, play out an assigned scenario by taking certain actions or asking certain questions, make observations about the business' appearance, sometimes make a purchase and/or return, and sometimes take photos. In-person shops are by far the most common type of mystery shop. In-person shops can be for literally any type of business that has a physical store location.

Remote shops are shops that are completed by phone, web, chat, instant messaging, etc. The shops may or may not require interaction with another person. Before accepting a remote shop be sure that you are comfortable with the technology skills required. Being able to access web pages, record calls, and take screenshots may be required for remote shops. While the surveys for remote shops are typically shorter and require less narratives, the shops also typically pay less than in-person shops. However, with the exploding growth of online commerce, online purchase shops are definitely becoming more common and more lucrative for shoppers. Remote shops also have the benefit of not requiring transportation expenses. For shoppers who do not have access to reliable transportation or are not able to leave home for whatever reason, remote shops may be a good choice.

Time Commitment and Flexibility

Can mystery shopping be a full-time job? This is probably the number one question I get from new and potential shoppers. The answer is...it depends. If you live in a large, heavily populated city then yes, there is a possibility that you could turn mystery shopping into a full-time job, although a lot of your "pay" will likely be in reimbursed food, merchandise, and services. But if you live in a suburban or rural area the chance of there being enough mystery shopping jobs close enough to you to take up 30-40 hours per week is slim, especially when you consider that there are probably at least a few other shoppers living in your area. This is why many people choose to do mystery shopping as a part-time addition to their regular full-time income.

There are other jobs out there that are similar to mystery shopping, such as merchandising or field agent work, and many part-time mystery shoppers fill in the income gap with these types of jobs. While this book does not cover merchandising or field agent work specifically, many of the companies who offer mystery shopping assignments also offer these types of assignments. You will also find many mystery shoppers discussing these types of assignments in some of the forums and resources provided later in this book.

Flexibility is probably the top reason that people become interested in mystery shopping. Many shop assignments will have time frames than span several days, so you can choose the day that works best for you to complete the shop, while some shops may require you visit on a specific day or at a certain time of day. There are also many shops that allow you to visit anytime the location is open. Some shops even allow (and encourage) you to bring kids, your spouse, or friends.

You will have the option to only apply for shops that fit into your schedule but it is important to note that this rarely means you can complete the shop whenever you want. Prior to applying for any shop, be sure to take note of the time frame in which the shop must be completed and the report submission deadline. Depending on the type and complexity of shop there may even be several submission deadlines you need to meet. Completing a shop outside of the allowed time frame or not submitting the report by the submission deadline are guaranteed ways to not get paid, and no one wants to work for free, so I highly suggest making sure that you can complete the shop and meet all deadlines before putting in an application for the shop. See more information below in Chapter 4: "What to Know: BEFORE Applying".

Avoiding Scams

Scams are, unfortunately, prevalent in the mystery shopping industry. Scammers will typically pose as a mystery shopping company offering work to potential shoppers. They will offer to send you money up front for completing a shop, typically with an outrageous payment for the shop. If you accept, they will send you a check for the payment amount they promised plus an additional amount that they will ask you to send back to them via money order. As soon as you cash the check, which does not belong to the scammer but instead and unsuspecting fraud victim, you are then liable to repay the full amount to the victim. This often leaves potential shoppers paying back money to the victim that they already sent to the scammers. The typical pay range for mystery shops is anywhere from $5 to $50 per shop. Most shops will fall in the $10 to $20 range. If a company is offering you $200 or $300 to complete a shop and you've never mystery shopped before, you can bet it's a scam.

The main lesson here is that a mystery shopping company will almost NEVER pay you before the shop. All payments are received after the shop is completed, submitted, and approved as per the company's payroll guidelines, which vary from company to company. It is also unusual for a company to provide you with funds ahead of time for a required purchase. Shoppers are typically required to pay for required purchases out of pocket and be reimbursed the approved amount along with their shop payment after the shop is completed and approved. I have only seen exceptions to this rule three times over the past 15+ years:

- One company provides shoppers with a gift card to the restaurant they are shopping beforehand to cover the required purchases. This is for a high-end restaurant so the required purchases are expensive, but this situation is still not typical. The restaurant being shopped most likely wants to see how employees handle customers paying with gift cards.
- Another company that specializes in amusement parks and attractions will provide the shopper with admission tickets for their assigned attraction beforehand so the shopper doesn't have to pay for admission out of their own pocket, but if the shop is not approved for any reason the shopper then owes the company the price of all tickets used.
- Another company that specializes in hospitality shops will make hotel stay arrangements ahead of time for shoppers assigned to shop that specific hotel. Once again, this is only for very high-end, expensive hotels and if the shop is not approved the shopper must repay the company the full room rate for each night they stayed.

In all three of these exceptions the locations being shopped are very expensive and it's very doubtful that any of these shops would be assigned to a brand new shopper. In any case, a reputable mystery shopping company would never send you cash or a check for payment prior to the shop.

Shop postings that contain lots of spelling and grammar errors sometimes indicate that the person posting the shop doesn't speak or write English well, which is a red flag that you might be dealing with a scammer. Use common sense...would Hilton hotels or Panera Bread post an available job on their websites with lots of spelling and grammar errors? Of course not, and they wouldn't hire a mystery shopping company that does either.

Another red flag that you may be dealing with a scammer is if they tell you the name of their client when offering you the job. Only companies that you are registered with as a shopper should send you shop offer emails that reveal client names and locations. These companies NEVER post their client's names on recruitment sites, forums, or social media, because this would violate pretty much every confidentiality rule in the industry. So that Facebook post by a mystery shopping company offering Starbucks shops that pay $200 each? That's a scam. A legitimate shop offer posting on social media would be more like: "Nationwide coffee chain shops available, $10 shop pay, $8 reimbursement, contact scheduler at scheduler@mysteryshoppingcompany.com or apply at www.mysteryshoppingcompany.com."

Confidentiality

I feel that a book about mystery shopping would not be complete without a note on confidentiality. It may go without saying that you shouldn't reveal yourself as a mystery shopper to store employees or other customers, but what about your friends and family? Is it okay to discuss what companies you are mystery shopping or what happens on your shops?

The answer is a hard NO. In fact, when you sign each company's Independent Contractor Agreement, or ICA, I can guarantee that there will be a section devoted entirely to you not discussing anything about your shop with anyone. The ICA is a legally binding agreement and violating it could land you anything from not getting paid for a shop to ending up in court (although the latter would be pretty extreme). You're also not typically allowed to post reviews on social media or other sites related to your experience at a business while mystery shopping or mention the clients you shop when applying with other mystery shopping companies. Just remember...when in doubt, shut your mouth!

All this confidentiality seems like it could lead to a pretty lonely work life, right? Not necessarily! With the uprising of internet forums and social media groups dedicated to the mystery shopping industry, shoppers worldwide now have whole communities of support. Links to several of these forums and groups are included in the text below.

Chapter 1 Summary

- Most mystery shops are in-person covert shops, where you physically visit a business location and do not reveal yourself as a mystery shopper to anyone

- Revealed mystery shops do require you to reveal your status as a mystery shopper at some point during the shop, usually near the end
- Remote mystery shops can be done in various ways, including via phone, website, email, instant messaging, and more
- While you may schedule mystery shops around your personal schedule you will still be required to complete the shop on the assigned date and meet other deadlines
- Scams are prevalent in the industry, so remember the following tips:
  - ☐ You will NOT be sent cash or a check BEFORE completing a mystery shop
  - ☐ Avoid available shop postings with poor spelling and grammar
  - ☐ Avoid available shop postings that reveal the end client's name or location
- Confidentiality is a pillar of the mystery shopping industry, so when in doubt...shut your mouth!

Chapter 2: . Finding Shops & Registering with Companies

Now that you know what mystery shops are it's time to find and complete your first shop!

Just 5 or 10 years ago searching for available mystery shops in your area was a pretty arduous task. Before you could even see what shops might be available you would have to register with each individual mystery shopping company (there are literally hundreds if not thousands in the US alone) and then search their job boards. Luckily, the convenience of technology has permeated the mystery shopping industry just like everything else, and searching for available shops is not so bad these days. Thanks to shop aggregators like Jobslinger, shop-search forums like Volition, and mobile apps like Gigspot, Prestomaps, and iSecretShop, you can see which companies offer shops in your area with just a few clicks. Many mystery shopping companies only operate in certain states or regions so being able to see which companies offer shops in your area before filling out lengthy applications is very helpful.

Some companies do not participate in any shop aggregator type services so you might still find that you need to check for available shops on their individual websites, but as a new shopper I would definitely suggest beginning with a shop aggregator service. This will allow you to quickly register with companies that offer shops in your area, start completing shops, build your experience, and put a little extra cash in your pocket!

Shopping Platforms

It's important to know that there are three main mystery shopping platforms - Sassie, Shopmetrics, and Prophet. Almost all mystery shopping companies use one of these three platforms. The rest use a variety of different programs or mobile apps. While the majority of this book focuses on Sassie and Shopmetrics platforms since they're the easiest to search and register for, some of the others are also discussed. I would highly recommend registering with companies that use a variety of platforms for the best chance at securing regular work.

Create a Mystery Shopping Email Address

To get started, create an email address to be solely used for mystery shopping purposes. Do not include the words shopper or mystery shopper or anything like that in this email address since you may need to use it while conducting a shop at some point and using these words will tip employees off that you're a mystery shopper. You can set this email address up using any reputable email service that you would like, such as Gmail or Yahoo. No need for anything fancy!

Autofill Setup

One of the easiest ways to fill in the info needed to register with companies quickly is using your browser's autofill feature. If you don't know how to use your browser's autofill feature you'll want to do an internet search for the name of your browser (Chrome, Safari, Firefox, etc.) and the words "autofill instructions". Remember when setting up your autofill profile to use the email address that you created just for mystery shopping.

Shop Aggregators

Sassie Companies via Jobslinger - http://www.jobslinger.com/

Searching Jobslinger

Once you have set up your email address for mystery shopping and set up your browser's autofill, head on over to www.jobslinger.com and click on "Create a New Account" to register for a free account. Use autofill to fill out the registration form and then double-check to be sure all the fields filled in correctly.

Once you're registered and logged in, click on the "Tools" drop-down menu just under the JobSlinger logo, then click "Search for Jobs". Enter your zip code in the box and adjust the mileage radius if you like (if you live in a very rural area you may want to increase your mileage radius, while those who live in urban settings may only want to go just a few miles from home), then click "Search" to see all the shops available from Sassie-affiliated companies within your specified radius. You can sort the results by the date posted, shop pay, distance from your specified ZIP code, or shop due date.

Each result will show you the title of the shop, the company offering the shop, the date posted, the shop pay, due date, and locations where the shop is offered. Some shops might be offered in multiple locations within your specified radius so you'll need to click on the number of locations just under the shop title to see each city where the shop is available.

On the far right of any shop result you'll see the Apply button. When you see a shop that you're interested in, just click the Apply button to go to that mystery shopping company's website and get more information or apply to complete the shop. You must be registered with the company prior to applying for any shop, but luckily registering is also pretty easy these days using your browser's autofill feature. We will cover registering in the next section.

If you don't see many results you can always adjust the mileage radius or search for shops by state. Searching by state can be a very useful function for shoppers living in rural areas. Living in an area that doesn't have many businesses, and therefore doesn't have many shops, may seem like a disadvantage, but this often means that mystery shopping companies have a hard time finding reliable shoppers there, so competition for shop is not as fierce. Some companies do not allow the same shopper to complete another shop at the same location until a certain amount of time has passed. This is known as rotation and causes mystery shopping companies to need multiple shoppers in the same area just to fill shops for one location. If you live in an area like this shops will often be bonused in an effort to get them filled before their deadlines. These bonuses can add a lot of extra cash to your pocket without any added expense, which is rare in highly populated area with lots of shoppers.

Jobslinger has many other features and benefits that shoppers will find very useful. Feel free to browse all of their features, including IC Pro certification (which is free to all shoppers) and the upgraded Jobslinger Pro membership service.

Registering with Sassie Companies

Search Jobslinger for shops in your area and make a list of which companies offer shops near you in which you are interested.

Click on the "Apply" button in the available shops results list to go to the company's website to register as a new shopper. You may also click on the "Tools" menu just under the Jobslinger logo and click on "Recruiterator. Here you will see a list of all of the companies who participate in the Sassie mystery shopping platform, which is the developer of Jobslinger. Find the companies on your list and click on the link to head over to that company's new shopper signup page.

Select your preferred language and click Go, then enter your email address and click Go again. Remember to use the email address you created for mystery shopping. Once the system verifies that you are not a currently registered shopper (if your email address is already registered it will ask you to login instead of signup) it will I asked you to read and sign the Independent Contractor Agreement, also known as an ICA. This is a legal document between you and the mystery shopping company verifying your status as a contractor and not an employee. This agreement will also set forth rules about confidentiality and expected shopper conduct. Review the agreement and sign per the instructions at the bottom of the page. Now you're ready to fill in your profile information (Note: occasionally you will be asked to fill in your profile before signing the ICA, it just depends on the company's setup) .

Click in the text box for first name and you should see your browser's autofill features pop up. Depending on your browser you may need to right click inside the box to see the autofill options. Choose the correct autofill entry and you should see the majority of the profile fields now filled in with your information. Go through and double-check that all the information populated correctly. There will still be a few questions that you have to answer manually, such as your height, hair color, marital status, etc.

Towards the bottom of the profile form it will ask you to enter your Social Security Number or Employer Identification Number. Entering this number is usually optional and is only used if you earn $600 or more with the company in one calendar year. According to IRS rules any independent contractor that earns more than $600 with a single company in a single calendar year is to be issued a 1099 for those earnings. This means that you will be required to claim this income on your income taxes and pay any taxes that may be due. If you are unsure about how your earnings will affect your taxes please consult with a tax preparer or certified accountant. Each person's tax situation is different so there would be no way to cover all the possible scenarios in this book. See the last chapter for more info on Tax Decisions.

The final question on your profile form will be which area codes you are willing to work in. You obviously want to put your home area code and any nearby area codes in these boxes. The number of area codes that you enter into these boxes (the max is 5) will depend on where you live. People in rural areas where area codes cover a large areas may only want to enter a couple of area codes, while those who live in an urban setting may want to use all five boxes. If you're unsure of what area codes are near you just do a quick internet search for "area code map" and the name of the state you live in. These maps are widely available for free on the internet and generally pretty accurate. I typically only use three or four of the boxes so I always like to fill in the last box with 800, just in case the company offers any phone shops under this prefix.

The company's privacy policy will be displayed on the very bottom of the page and you will be asked to check a box confirming that you have read it.

Now just click "Save" and you should see a green confirmation that your profile was saved. Just under this confirmation near the top of your profile, make sure that the field "Get Shop Offer Emails" is set to

"On". If it's not, change it to "On" and click "Save" again at the bottom of the page.

Some Sassie-based companies require you to also fill out what is called an "Extended Shopper Profile". There will be a link to this near the top of your profile page and if it's not completed it will usually have an icon that is outlined in red. Click on the link to open up a separate window with the extended profile questions. You won't be able to use autofill to answer these questions since they're usually different for each company. They may also ask you to upload a photo or copy of a driver's license in order to verify that you qualify for age limited shops. Fill in all of this information as applicable and click "Save" to save the extended profile and close the separate window. When back on your standard profile page you may need to refresh the page in order to verify that your extended profile saved correctly.

Now you're all set up to receive email shop offers and to search the job board for this company! Repeat the steps for each company that you found on Jobslinger that offers shops in your area. After you register with each company, be sure to link them to your Jobslinger account by clicking on the "Tools" menu, then "Connections". Here you'll be able to enter your login information for each Sassie company to link them to Jobslinger and streamline the application process. While the application process can be repetitive, making use of your browser's autofill feature will lighten the load a lot.

Searching Sassie Company Job Boards

To search a Sassie company's Job Board, just click on "Job Board" near the top of the page while logged in to the company's shopper website. Adjust the mileage radius to your desired area, choose to search either the radius around your home address, the radius around your current location (you'll have to allow this site to access your location for the current location search to work), or the radius around a different address that you specify in the text box. You can enter a full address here or just a zip code. Then click "Search" and you'll see all the standard shops that that company is offering within your search parameters (Non-standard shops are usually by invite only and not displayed on the job boards).

Now you can easily see more details about the shop and put in an application by either clicking on the shop's location pin in the map or using the links on the right side of each result listed under the map. Each shop result listed will show you the start and end date for the shop, the company to be shopped, location and other contact information, distance from the area that you searched, shop payment, shop reimbursement, any shop bonus that might be added, and a short description of the shop. This description typically includes the contact information for the shop's scheduler, who is the person that manages the scheduling and completion of the shop. If you have questions about the shop that are not answered in the description feel free to contact the shop scheduler for more info. Shop schedulers are usually more than happy to answer your questions about a shop but be prepared to wait 24 to 48 hours to hear back from some of them. Others are very responsive and you may have your answer within a few minutes.

Once you have found a shop that you want to complete just click on the "Apply" link to go to the shop's application page. Again you will see all the information about the shop listed and a calendar near the bottom of the page where you can choose the date that you intend to complete the shop. There may be some supplemental questions next to the calendar that must be answered for your application to be submitted. Once you have filled out all this information just click on "Apply for this Shop" and your application will be sent to the shop scheduler. You will be notified via email if your application is accepted or rejected. You can also monitor the status of your applications by logging into the company's website and clicking ping "My Apps" in the header menu at the top right of the page.

Since there's a lot of consistency in how the New Shopper Sign-up is laid out and their shops are easy to find I definitely suggest signing up with Sassie-based companies first. However, there are many really great mystery shopping companies out there that do not use the Sassie system, so don't stop here!. Read on for information about some of the lesser-used mystery shopping platforms, proprietary platforms, and how to sign up with these companies efficiently.

Shopmetrics Companies via MS Job Board - https://www.msjobboard.com/

Similar to Jobslinger is MS Job Board, which is the shop aggregator for companies who use the Shopmetrics platform. Just like Jobslinger, not all Shopmetrics companies participate in MS Job Board, but it's still a great place to search for shops from multiple companies in one place.

Search MS Job Board

Go to the website at https://www.msjobboard.com/ and click on the "Sign Up" tab. Enter the requested details or use autofill to register. After registering you will be sent an email with your username and password. Be sure to check your email's Spam or Junk folder if you don't see this email in your inbox within a few minutes. Once you find the email, read it over for some general info on how MS Job Board works, then click on the link to go back to the website. Enter your username and password as found in the email (I suggest double clicking the password, then press Ctrl + C to copy it exactly (long press then tap Copy on a mobile device), since it is case-sensitive) and log in.

The first thing you'll want to do is change your password to something more familiar unless you want to search for the intro email every time you need to log in. Just click on "My Settings" at the top right of the screen, then click "Change Password". Change your password to anything you'd like, or use a password manager to create secure, unique passwords for all your site logins. There are several free password managers available online and through the app stores on mobile devices.

Now that you've changed your password, it's time to complete your profile. Click on "My Profile" in the vertical menu bar on the left side of the screen. Now fill in all the details of your profile. You'll notice once you begin registering with individual Shopmetrics companies that this profile is standard across all Shopmetrics companies. Once you have filled in all the profile information click "Save" at the bottom of the page.

Now you're ready to search for shops! Just click on "My Job Board" on the top of the vertical menu bar on the left side of the page. The Job Board defaults to 20 miles around your home zip code (known as your "Coverage Area"). For rural shoppers, you'll probably want to expand this area beyond the 20 mile radius to see more available shops. Just click the radio button for "Search by Postal Code and Distance", then adjust the mileage radius to whatever you would like. You can also search around different zip codes if you plan to be outside of your home area.

What I really like about MS Job Board is:

- You can view a company's available jobs without actually linking the company to your account
- They offer robust search filters
- You can view results on a list, map, or in calendar view

Once you've searched and found a shop you are interested in click on the shop's name. You'll see the shop's basic details pop up. Review the shop details and if you're still interested click the "Apply" button at the bottom of the popup box. You'll then be prompted to either go directly to the company's website to apply or to link the company to MS Job Board so you can apply directly from here. You must have a username and password for the company prior to linking it to MS Job Board, so if you don't yet, go ahead and click "Continue without linking this site" to go to the company's website and register. Once you've registered with the company feel free to come back to MS Job Board and link them. See the next section on registering with companies for more info on finding Shopmetrics companies to register with using MS Job Board (and other resources).

Registering with Shopmetrics Companies

The process for using MS Job Board to help find and register with Shopmetrics companies is similar to the process for Sassie companies via Jobslinger.

After registering for MS Job Board, use the instructions in the last section to do a quick search for shops in your area. Once you've found a shop you're interested in, go ahead and click on the shop's name to bring up the shop details popup. Review the details and if you're still interested, click on "Apply Now" at the bottom of the popup. You will now see a popup asking you to either visit the company's website directly or link the company to your MS Job Board account. Go ahead and click "Continue without linking this site" to go to the company's website and register as a shopper. Use autofill to make registering easier!

Repeat these steps for each job posting your find on MS Job Board to register with each company. After you register with each company, return to MS Job Board and click on "My Linked Sites" on the left side vertical menu near the bottom. Now click on the name of the company you just registered with and enter your login info for that company. Now you'll be able to apply for jobs with this company directly through MS Job Board without having to visit each company's website!

**Note: Companies that offer shops on mobile apps like Gigspot may redirect you to the app when you attempt to apply for their shops or register, and this is completely normal.

Searching Shopmetrics Company Job Boards

Once you're finished registering on a Shopmetrics company's website, feel free to search their job board. Make sure you're logged in to your shopper account and click "Open Opportunities" on the left side of the page. You'll now see some search filter options at the top of the page under the header. The search will default to whatever search radius and zip code you set in your profile, so you may want to adjust this to see shops in different areas and click "Update Filter". I personally find it easier to search by state on the Shopmetrics platform, so I clear out the zip code, enter my state's two-letter abbreviation in the "State" search filter box, then click "Update Filter".

Browse through the search results listed under the search filter options and click on the Info icon next to the name of each shop for more details in a popup box. After reviewing these details, along with the dates and pay rate shown in the search results, click on the "Apply" button at the far right of the shop result in which you are interested. A popup box will appear asking you to include a comment explaining why you would be a good fit for this shop and the date you plan to complete the shop. No date range is allowed here so you must choose one specific date and stick to it. Shops cannot always be rescheduled, so be careful when choosing your date. Now just click the "Apply" button and your application will be sent to the shop's scheduler. Monitor your mystery shopping email inbox for an email from the company either assigning or rejecting you for this shop. Since companies don't always send rejection notices, you can also monitor the status of your applications by logging into the company's shopper website and clicking on "My Applications" on the left side of the page.

Prophet

Unfortunately, Prophet does not offer a shop aggregator, but they do have a page that lists different companies that use the Prophet platform at https://shoppershare.archondev.com/. Registering with each individual company, searching their job boards, and monitoring your email for shop offers will be required for these companies. This is a much more hit-and-miss approach because there's no way to tell if the company offer shops in your area until after you have registered with them unless the company posts their shop offerings on forums or Facebook groups. Since you might end up wasting some time registering with companies that are not very active or do not operate in your area, I would suggest monitoring the Sassie and Shopmetrics shop aggregators already mentioned, plus the forums and Facebook groups discussed below, for job offerings in your area and registering with the companies that post on those first. Then, whenever you have some extra time, search through mystery shopping company lists, like this one provided by Prophet, and do some "cold" applications. Lists of mystery shopping companies can also found on many of the sites mentioned below, including MSPA, Volition, Mystery Shop Forum, Mystery Shopping Solutions, and more.

MSPA - https://mspa-americas.org/

The MSPA, or Mystery Shopping Professional's Association, is an international professional trade organization dedicated to the progress and improvement of the mystery shopping industry. They specialize in hosting conferences for industry professionals and providing levels of shopper certification. If you want to take your shopping to the next level, consider some of their training courses, which covers everything from the very basics to advanced video shopping.

MSPA also offers an "Opportunity Board" where members can search for available shops. You can become a basic Independent Contractor member for free, or upgrade to the $30 IC Plus membership for some extra perks.

After you register and login you can access the "Opportunity Board" from the footer at the bottom of almost any page. They have robust search options but don't be surprised if you find a lot of overlap with Jobslinger and many of the other search methods. Also like Jobslinger, you cannot view available jobs on a map, which I find inconvenient.

Shadowshopper -
https://www.shadowshopper.com/

Shadowshopper is a site dedicated to allowing schedulers from any company post available jobs. They offer a free Bronze membership for shoppers or a Gold membership for as little as $6.95 for 30 days. The Bronze membership will only get you week-old, limited access to available shops while the Gold membership promises exclusive, early access to the best shops. I do not have a Gold membership so I cannot speak to it's value, but the shops available with a Bronze membership have a lot of overlap with other search methods, and week-old shops will almost surely be filled by other shoppers by the time you apply. I also do not like that you cannot view available shops on a map and many of the emails I receive from them are from survey companies and other non-mystery shopping or merchandising related companies.

Shadowshopper offers its own shopper certification testing that you can choose to complete if you wish. The free test offered to Bronze memberships covers the basics of mystery shopping and is all good info to know for new shoppers.

Mobile Apps

Using mobile apps to find and/or complete mystery shops are still a relatively new idea in the industry, however, companies who do use mobile apps are seeing improvements in shopper productivity and accuracy. When the shopper is able to enter reports and upload photos directly into the app just after leaving the store there's much less chance of the shopper forgetting important details. Mobile devices have also allow shoppers to prove that they were really at the shop location using GPS locating apps such as Geoverify. Many mobile apps also allow you to register with many different companies that participate in the app with just a few clicks, but others may require you to register with the company that created the app on a desktop or laptop prior to being able to access the app.

Gigspot - https://www.gigspot.com/

One of the best shop aggregator apps is Gigspot. Instead of having to fill out application info 50 different times for 50 different mystery shopping companies, you can fill out your profile one time in Gigspot and then accept each company's agreement with just a few clicks. You will then have access to all of that companies available shops in your area. Try it out by going to the play store or iTunes, depending on your mobile device, then downloading the Gigspot app. (You can also visit their website on a desktop or laptop at https://www.gigspot.com/)

Once downloaded, just fill in your profile information and then tap on the "Companies" tab at the bottom right of the screen. Here you'll see a list of all the companies that participate in the Gigspot app. You'll be able to tap on each company and sign their shopper agreement right in the app. Then feel free to apply for any available shops this company may offer. Even if you haven't signed a company's shopper agreement yet you can still view the available shops from that company in the app and then sign the agreement just before applying.

Remember, the Gigspot app is based on your device's current location, so if you want to search for available shops in an area far away from where you are, such as if you plan to go on vacation next week and want to see what shops might be available in Miami, move the slider from "Near Home" to "Search" on the Job Board page in the app and you'll be able to search any area you wish. The first entry shown is typically remote shops, followed by traditional in-person shops.

iSecretShop - https://isecretshop.com/

iSecretShop is another great shop aggregator app that many companies participate in. This one operates very similarly to Gigspot. You just fill in your profile info one time and then you can accept shopper agreements from all of the companies that participate in the iSecretShop app. iSecretShop also features a separate section for web/phone shops only.

PrestoMaps - https://insta.prestometrics.com/site/Map

PrestoMaps is one of my favorite shop aggregator apps. While many of the shops shown on PrestoMaps are from Sassie-based companies and therefore will also be posted on Jobslinger, the PrestoShops posted on PrestoMaps are unique to this app and pay incredibly fast - within 48 hours! These are a great way to grab some quick cash and the survey reports are typically very easy to fill out.

Proprietary Apps

Some companies develop their own apps that only feature shops from that particular company. Second to None and Ipsos come to mind as larger mystery shopping companies that provide their own dedicated app to shoppers. These companies allow shoppers to use the app or their website to apply for and submit shops. This gives shoppers more flexibility since not everyone even has a desktop or laptop, but almost everyone has a smartphone. Proprietary apps will have different instructions for accessing and searching for available jobs, but should be similar to the apps already mentioned.

All mystery shopping mobile apps should be available to download via iTunes or the Play Store.

Forums

Another great way to search for available shops in your area is through forums dedicated to the mystery shopping industry. Just remember that if you choose to register with any of the forums, use the email address you created for mystery shopping and also an alias username. The forums are a great place to ask questions and vent about shopper problems but you don't want every scheduler out there knowing exactly who you are because your name is your username. Trust me, schedulers and mystery shopping companies monitor these forums constantly so using an alias is your best bet.

Volition - http://forum.volition.com/

One of the oldest and most well-known mystery shopping forums is Volition. If it's something related to mystery shopping you'll definitely find it here. While they haven't always had a shop search feature on Volition, some years ago they added it and it's been a blessing for shoppers and companies alike. You can access their "Job Openings & Recruitment Ads" forum at http://jobs.volition.com/exec/sfs/jobboard. Now any mystery shopping company, regardless of what platform they use, can post their available shops to the Volition forums for shoppers all over the world to see. You don't have to be a registered user of Volition and you don't have to be registered with any specific mystery shopping company to view anything posted on Volition. Just like with Jobslinger, once you find a shop posting that you're interested in just click on the link to go to the company's website, get more information, and apply. You'll need to register with the company before applying for any shop, but again, this is pretty easy with autofill and only necessary one time.

In addition to their awesome "Job Openings" forum, Volition has a wealth of information in all of their other mystery shopping and merchandising related forums. Volition is where I got my start in mystery shopping and I would HIGHLY suggest that all new shoppers explore what they have to offer, although their forums are not quite as active now as they used to be.

Mystery Shop Forum -
https://www.mysteryshopforum.com/

Mystery Shop Forum is another great resource for shoppers looking for available shops and to connect with other shoppers. This forum functions essentially the same as the Volition and allows companies to post their available shops regardless of company or platform affiliation. You will need to be a registered user on the Mystery Shop Forum website in order to search the available shops, but I would recommend registering anyway to take advantage of these very active forums. Don't forget to use an alias!

Mystery Shopping Solutions -
https://www.mystshopsol.com/shoppers/shopper_menu.asp

Mystery Shopping Solutions is the final mystery shopping forum I'll mention here. While this forum doesn't have any of the bells and whistles of other forums, I like its streamlined approach for viewing available shops. As a shopper you are required to register and fill out a profile before viewing their job board. After registering, search for available shops by state, ZIP code and mileage radius, or shops that can be done from anywhere. Just like the others, just click on the link in the shop posting to get more info and apply for the shop. Mystery Shopping Solutions isn't as widely used as the other forums, but you can still find a gem here every once in a while.

Facebook Groups -
https://www.facebook.com/groups

Facebook groups are another great way to search for available shops. Do not use your personal Facebook account to sign up for mystery shopping Facebook groups! Create a totally separate Facebook account using the email address you created for mystery shopping. I would also not recommend putting your actual photo as your profile picture or really divulging any information about yourself other than maybe the state or country you live in and a short bio. As long as you don't have any identifying information in the Facebook profile about yourself you should be fine to include that you're a mystery shopper in the bio if you choose. Just be very careful about not revealing your identity as a mystery shopper. You would be surprised at how many business owners monitor these Facebook groups and forums to try to identify mystery shoppers coming into their locations. If you've got your photo and the name of the exact town or neighborhood that you live in in this profile it could be easy for a local business owner to find you and compromise any shop that you might perform at their business. It's better to err on the side of caution and use a less-is-more approach to your mystery shopping Facebook account.

Once you set up your account it's time to start joining groups. In addition to groups created by individual mystery shopping companies there are also independent groups created for the sole purpose of posting available job offers. The list below shows the names of some of the most popular mystery shopping groups on Facebook, but new groups are being created all the time! I would highly recommend doing a groups search on Facebook using the words "mystery shopping" and the state or area that you live in. This may show you some local mystery shopping groups that will hopefully have available shops in your area posted. For the groups shown below, just do a Facebook search for the group's name and request permission to join. Once your request is accepted make sure to turn on notifications from the group so you'll see shop postings as soon as possible. The early bird gets the worm when applying for mystery shops!

Facebook groups created by individual mystery shopping companies may require you to be a registered shopper of that company before they approve your Facebook group request. Just go to that company's official website and sign up as a new shopper to gain access to their exclusive Facebook group.

Once some of your group join requests are approved, go ahead and open up that group's page. Use the search box near the top of the feed to search for your city's name and zip code. You will also want to search for any cities that you are willing to travel to for a shop. Check the details of any posts that come up, including the post date to be sure it's recent, and if you're still interested in the shop follow the instructions in the post to apply. Once you've checked out all posts in one group, simply move on to the next and search the exact same way. You can keep up with which groups have approved you from the Groups page, which can be accessed by clicking "Groups" under "Explore" from your Facebook news feed.

Proprietary Platforms

While the vast majority of mystery shopping companies use one of the three main platforms that I've mentioned above, there are still a few holdouts who use their own proprietary systems. Again, there's no way to see what shops these companies have available without registering first unless they post to forums or Facebook groups. Just like with the Prophet platform companies, you may want to monitor forums and Facebook groups for postings before spending time on an application with these companies.

While the shop aggregators make things easy, I definitely recommend taking the time to register with companies that don't use aggregators when you have some extra time. You may be surprised at how many shop offers you get from a company that uses their own proprietary system. I've listed a few companies below that use proprietary systems and are quite popular:

A Closer Look - http://www.a-closer-look.com/

Second to None - https://www.second-to-none.com/

International Service Check - https://www.internationalservicecheck.com/en/evaluator

Avoid Searching for Companies using Internet Search

You might think that just searching for "mystery shopping companies" using internet search like Google or Bing would be a good way to find companies. I would like to urge you not to do this. While many reputable companies do advertise using online search engines many scammers also advertise this way by posing as reputable companies. The scam advertisements copy the name and information of a reputable company and also appear to spoof that company's website URL. Use the resources I have identified above to identify and connect with reputable mystery shopping companies. if you are dealing with a company that you cannot find any information about using Jobslinger, MSPA, Shadowshopper, mystery shopping forums, or mystery shopping Facebook groups, they may very well be a scam company. If the company is using the name of a reputable mystery shopping company but other red flags have made you suspicious, simply go to the real company's official website and contact them via phone. They will be more than happy to let you know if the information that you are receiving is legitimate or from an illegitimate source. Overall, use common sense and remember, if it seems too good to be true, it probably is.

Chapter 2 Summary

- There are three main mystery shopping platforms - Sassie, Shopmetrics, and Prophet
- Create an email address and autofill profile dedicated to mystery shopping before you begin searching for shops
- Start your search with shop aggregators, which make finding shops from multiple companies very easy. Aggregators can be websites, like Jobslinger or MS Job Board, or mobile apps, like Gigspot and PrestoMaps.
- Find available shops and stay connected with the mystery shopping community using forums and Facebook Groups dedicated to the industry
- Some companies still use proprietary platforms on their websites or apps, so be prepared to learn a slightly different platform when you work with these companies
- Using internet search to find mystery shopping companies can leave you open to scams, so use the sources I've provided in this book instead

Chapter 3: Monitoring Emails

Once you start registering with companies the emails will start rolling in...and you'll really start appreciating having a separate email address! While it's always a good idea to keep an eye on company job boards as well, pretty much all companies advertise to their registered shoppers via email. Whenever a scheduler has a shop or shops they need filled, they usually send an email out about the shop to registered shoppers. How they choose which shoppers to send the email out to varies by company and scheduler. Schedulers can send emails out to shoppers within a certain radius of the shop location, statewide, nationwide, worldwide, or use some other specific criteria to filter out just the shoppers it wants to reach.

For example, a gas station shop in a small town maybe advertise to shoppers within 20 miles of the gas station's location or to every shopper in the same state as the gas station. In contrast, a restaurant shop behind security at a major airport will likely be advertised nationwide or only to shoppers who have specified that they travel via air frequently. This is why it's important to fill out your shopper profile questions accurately so you are considered for all the shops for which you are eligible.

The format of the emails you will receive about available shops varies based on the platform and company. However, almost all emails will contain the following information: information about the company offering the shop, a brief description of the shop, a list of locations where the shop is being offered, and the link to click on for more information and to apply for the shop.

Companies who use the Sassie or Shopmetrics platform typically use the same standard email format. The Sassie format lists the cities where available shops are located grouped by state. This list is always near the bottom of the email and allows you to quickly scan and see if the shop is available in any of the cities or towns you frequent. Always be sure to read the shop description before applying... just because the shop is being offered in your city doesn't mean but you're automatically eligible. Some shops have restrictions including age, gender, clothing size, household income, and more. This is why it's important to always read the shop description both in the email and on the company's website before applying. See the following chapter on what to know before you apply for a shop.

Occasionally you may get a direct, one-to-one email from a scheduler offering you a shop. These emails will typically require you to reply directly to the email to be assigned to the shop. Having direct communication with a scheduler is nice because you avoid the normal competition for shops and get a direct line into being assigned. Building this type of relationship with company schedulers can be very profitable for your mystery shopper business.

You're going to need to monitor your email frequently for new shop offers. The sooner you see and can respond to shop offer emails, the better your chances of being assigned to shops. If you are able to access your mystery shopping email on your smartphone device and possibly activate notifications this would be ideal. If not, I recommend checking your email at least once a day and more often when possible. Checking your email any less than daily is not ideal because shop offer emails become outdated quickly as shops are assigned and new shops are added, so clicking on links in emails that are days old will frequently lead you to a shop that has already been assigned to another shopper. This can be very disappointing if you were very interested in the shop or it was for a location where you needed to make a purchase anyway. The early bird definitely gets the worm when it comes to monitoring emails for shop offers! (Are you noticing a trend here?)

Mobile mystery shopping apps have taken away some of the need for monitoring email since these apps will notify you via device notification when new shops are available in your area. You can then get more information and apply for the shop directly from your device. The downfall of this is that you won't get notifications about shops outside of your home area.

On the other side of this coin, there are the companies that do not advertise shops via email at all. They require their register shoppers to log in to their websites to view available shops. Information about how shop offers are made should be included in the Independent Contractor Agreement that you signed when registering with the company or with some of their orientation materials for new shoppers. When in doubt, don't hesitate to email a company and ask them about their shop offer policies.

While you can't rely on just one method to see all available shops, monitoring email is still the best way to stay on top of shop offers and increase your chances of being assigned.

Chapter 3 Summary

- Email is still the best way to receive and respond to mystery shop offers
- Check email at least daily to stay on top of current offerings and respond in a timely fashion
- Shop offer emails may be formatted differently depending on the company that sends them and what shopping platform they use
- Shop schedulers use different methods to decide which shoppers will receive an available shop offer
- Mobile apps have taken away some of the need for email monitoring since you can now receive shop offer notifications on your mobile device as soon as the shop is posted
- Some companies do not use email at all for shop offers, so you will need to check these companies job boards on their websites frequently for new shop offers

Chapter 4: What to Know: BEFORE Applying

Shop Purpose

The shop's purpose is arguably the most important information you will need to know about the shop before applying. The shop's purpose will be outlined in the shop's description, both in any email offers you receive and also on the company's website. It is incredibly important not to assume that you know what a shop's purpose is just because of what type of location it is or where it's located. For example, you may assume that the purpose of a shop at a popular retail clothing store is to evaluate the store's customer service when it could really be just to make sure that signage about the store's new rewards program is displayed on the sales floor. It is important to read the shop description completely before applying. If you are unsure about anything you should contact the scheduler identified in the shop description with questions before applying. If a scheduler is not identified in the shop description then try going to the help section on the company's website and finding contact information there. If all else fails you can always just pick up the phone and call the company and they can direct you to the correct person.

Submission Requirements/Collateral

You also need to know exactly what you will be required to submit for your shop to be approved and payment to be issued. Submission requirements can be anything from photo evidence to receipts to audio recordings of phone conversations with staff. Most companies outline the shops submission requirements clearly in the shop's description but if you are unsure always ask before applying! If you accept a shop that requires you to submit a receipt for a purchase up to $5 but you are unable to make this purchase then your shop will not be approved and you will not be paid. Likewise, if you accept the shop that requires you to submit a video recording of your interaction with the location's staff but you do not own or know how to operate covert video recording equipment, your shop will not be approved and you will not be paid. Some companies may call the submission requirements collateral or use some other term but almost all shops will require you to submit at least one item of this type.

Deadlines

All shops have a deadline, and missing it in most cases means you won't be paid. Some shops will give you a date range in which you can complete the shop, while others will give you just one date on which the shop is to be completed. It is crucial that you complete the shop within the assigned date range or on the assigned date.

Some shops may also require your visit to be in a certain time of day, such as breakfast hours for a restaurant shop or after 9pm for a late-night bar shop. With any shop, visiting the location when they are not open or outside of the assigned time range will invalidate your shop and you'll have to return on a different date or have the shop cancelled entirely, which means you won't be paid. Do the research ahead of time and make sure that the location is open when you are available to visit. Google will be your best friend for finding location hours. Occasionally the hours given to you in the shop instructions won't match the hours the location is open. In that case, you'll need to contact the shop's scheduler to find out how to proceed. Don't just assume that you can visit whenever the location is open...it's always best to ask the scheduler.

Once you've completed the shop, you'll also have a deadline to submit your report. Most companies ask that you submit your report within 12 to 24 hours, although some may request it immediately after leaving the location and others may give you up to 48 hours to submit. It's very important that you are aware of and adhere to this submission deadline. The company's standard submission deadline will be outlined in the Independent Contractor Agreement and new shopper orientation materials. If the shop submission deadline deviates from the company standard then the specific shop submission deadline information should be contained in the shop's description. Again, when in doubt, email or call the scheduler for clarification.

Payment

Getting paid is what we're all in it for, and it's crucially important to know EVERYTHING about the shop's proposed payment BEFORE submitting an application. Over the last 15 years I have lost money on a shop more than once because I didn't go over the payment details closely enough when applying. Payments for shops usually consists of a combination of three pay types: Shop Fee, Reimbursement, and Bonus Pay. The Shop Fee may also be referred to as "Base Pay" and Bonus Pay may be referred to as "Incentive Pay" or something similar.

All shops will offer either a Shop Fee or Reimbursement (if a purchase is required). Most shops offer both, however, shops that don't require a purchase will have a Shop Fee alone and shops that require a purchase will occasionally offer Reimbursement only. In addition to the Shop Fee and any Reimbursement, the shop may also have Bonus Pay. Bonus Pay is usually included for hard-to-fill shops that have a deadline coming up soon.

When considering whether or not the payment offered is sufficient, think about the following questions:

1. Is this a place I intend to shop at anyway? Will I basically be receiving an item or service for free that I would have paid for? If this is the case, you may want to strongly consider applying for the shop. Always double-check the shop description to make sure that the item or service you wish to purchase is covered by the

53

reimbursement and suitable for the shop's purpose.

2. How far is the shops location from my home and or work? Will I encounter any transportation costs such as parking, tolls, etc? Will visiting the shop's location require me to travel outside of my normal route? If the Shop Fee doesn't cover your travel expenses and it's not a place you shop anyway, it's probably not worth it.

3. What's the estimated amount of time to do the shop? A shop that requires 30 minutes of your time, not including time to write up the report, and only pays $5 really isn't worth it.

4. Am I available to commit that amount of time during the time range and on the date the shop is to be completed? For example, if it's a weekday lunch shop at a restaurant about 20 minutes one-way from your work, will you have time to get there, do the shop without rushing, and get back to work before your lunch break is over? It's always a good idea to overestimate time just in case you run into any issues.

5. How many questions are on the shop survey report? How much narrative is required? True-False and multiple-choice questions are easy to answer quickly, but narrative sections can take quite a bit of time, especially if you're not a strong writer. You'll need to consider how much time you think filling out the shop survey

report will take in addition to the actual time spent completing the shop and travel time.

6. Will the reimbursement amount realistically cover the cost of the required purchases? It may sound crazy, but sometimes the reimbursement amount just barely covers the absolute cheapest items at the location. For example, the reimbursement for a restaurant dinner shop may only cover the cheapest entree on the menu. If you don't happen to like that entree then you'll be stuck covering the difference between the cost of it and the cost of the entree you actually wish to order. This can be unappealing for a restaurant you wouldn't typically dine at anyway. Also, some shops may offer a ridiculously low reimbursement amount. Gas station shops are notorious for this. I've actually seen reimbursement amounts as low as $1. They are basically just wanting you to get a receipt to prove that you were at the shop location, but there's better ways to verify this and almost nothing in a gas station these days cost less than a dollar. Especially not anything you might actually want to buy. Don't feel bad about turning down a shop because they're being cheapskates with the reimbursement.

All of the payment information about a shop will be given to you up-front before you apply. If it's not, then you may want to reconsider applying for shops with the company. Remember, you will ALMOST NEVER be paid up-front for a shop, and if you are, it will NEVER be with cash or check. I've only seen shop prepayments in the form of a gift card for the specific location or tickets for attractions.

Knowing when you'll be paid is just as important as knowing how much. Most mystery shopping companies pay shoppers in the month following the month the shop was completed. For example, a shop completed in the month of May would be paid sometime in June. Not all companies follow this payment schedule, but the majority do.

Companies may pay shoppers via Paypal (most common), direct deposit, or paper check. Some companies offer some of the smaller electronic payment options but these are not common.You will definitely want to set up a Paypal account using your mystery shopping email address in order to receive payments for shops. You may also want to consider opening a separate bank account for your shop earnings and expenses, since you are technically running a mystery shopping business of your very own. Consult a financial planner or accountant for more information on what is required where you live.

Testing/Certifications

Each company you work with will have tests that you may have to complete before applying for or completing a shop. These tests (also known as certifications, depending on the company) check your knowledge of the shop requirements. Before taking the test, you will be given all the study materials, usually as a PDF file or web page. Read this study material from top to bottom, then keep it open while you work on the actual test. You may have to open it as a new tab or download the PDF to your device and then open it with your device's PDF viewer in order to have it and the test open at the same time. While you're taking the test, refer back to the study PDF to be sure you get every question correct. Can't find the answer you're looking for? Use the "Search" or "Find in Page" feature on your device's browser (Ctrl + F on a desktop or laptop) to quickly search the PDF or web page for the answer.

The number of questions you must answer correctly varies by company and test. Some companies will require 100% correct, while others may only require 80 or 90%. Luckily, most of these tests allow you at least two attempts to get the required number of questions correct. Once you have completed the test successfully one time, you won't have to take it again unless the company makes major changes to the shop instructions. In that case, you'll be notified of the need to retake the test in the shop offer email and in the shop's description. Also, the test will only qualify you for the one specific shop, so the company will likely have different tests for different shops. For example, Company ABC offers shops at a popular fast food restaurant and also at a small, specialty boutique. These shops have very different purposes and instructions, so Company ABC has a different test for each of these shops.

*Note: Some companies may also require new shoppers to take a test when registering or before applying for shops. This test typically covers the very basics of mystery shopping and it should not be difficult. The company will provide you with study materials prior to taking any test.

So now that you know what to look for when deciding which shops to apply for, head back over to your email and start browsing through shop offers. Find one you're interested in, check the shop description and payment info thoroughly, triple-check the dates and times, and see if any tests are required. Does everything check out? Then go ahead and hit that Apply link, sit back, and keep your fingers crossed that you're assigned!

Chapter 4 Summary

- It's important to know some important details about a shop before you submit an application
- Do not assume that you know a shop's purpose based on what type of store it is or where it is located...it could be very different!
- Mystery shops typically require at least one, but often more, pieces of collateral to prove you were in the correct location on the correct date and time
- Collateral can include receipts, photos, business cards, a code from a geoverification app, or others
- All shops must be completed on the correct date at the correct time - be sure this fits into your schedule before you apply

- All shops must be submitted within a certain time frame after completion - this is the submission deadline and it varies by company
- Some shops may have multiple parts and therefore multiple submission deadlines
- All companies issue payment for completed and approved shops differently...know the company's pay policy before you apply!
- Many mystery shops requires shoppers to pass a one-time test or certification before applying for an available shop. There will usually be a different test for each shop type since different shops have different purposes and requirements.

Chapter 5: What to Know: Before the Shop

Immediately Upon Assignment

So you've put in some applications for shops and before you know it an "Assigned" email hits your inbox. Congratulations! You're on your way to completing your very first mystery shop!

Confirm Shop Details

Immediately upon receiving your assignment email, you need to double-check all the shop details and read EVERYTHING associated with the shop. Most Sassie-based shops require you to confirm the assignment when you receive the assignment email by clicking on a confirmation link. If your shop is with a Sassie company, go ahead and click on the confirmation link in the assignment email to go to the company's website and confirm that you intend to complete the shop on the assigned date and time. While you're already on the site, login so you can review the shop's instructions and forms. If you're shopping for a company that doesn't use the Sassie platform, skip the confirmation step and go directly to the company's website to login (there should be a link to the company's website in the assignment email).

Most company sites will take you directly to your assigned shops page when you login, although it's called different things on different platforms. Sassie calls it the "Shop Log", Prophet calls it "My Visits", and Shopmetrics uses "Inbox". Companies that use proprietary software platforms may call it a variety of things.

After you login, go ahead and click on the name of the shop which you were just assigned. You should be able to see all the shop details, including date, time, address, a link to the instructions ,and shop survey form. Plug the exact address into your maps app or GPS so you're 100% on the shop's exact location. Don't forget to include the road direction in the address if applicable - 101 N Broadway Blvd and 101 S Broadway Blvd are different addresses and will likely take you to two very different locations.

Verify that all the shop details are correct. If they're not, contact the shop scheduler immediately.

Read ALL Shop Instructions/Guidelines

Now click the link in the shop details to open the shop instructions (sometimes referred to as "guidelines"). Read the instructions thoroughly from top to bottom, more than once if needed. You need to understand every part of the instructions in order to complete the shop correctly.

Read ENTIRE Shop Survey Form

After you finish reviewing the shop instructions, go back to the shop details screen on the company website and you should see a link to open the actual shop survey form that you will be filling out after the shop. (Occasionally you may not be able to see this form until closer to your actual shop date, and if this is the case you should see a message with the date that the shop survey form will be available.) Click the link to open the shop survey form and read the entire form from top to bottom, more than once if needed. Read each and every question on the form, even if you don't think it applies to your shop. All the questions might not apply, but it's important to familiarize yourself with any situation that may arise.

Additional Instructions

After you finish reviewing the shop survey form, go back to the shop details page. On some platforms, including Sassie, additional instructions may be attached to the shop details with a yellow sticky-note icon or some other form of marker. Click on this icon or marker to review these additional instructions, which typically override the general shop instructions. Also keep an eye out for emails or phone calls from the shop scheduler with further instructions or clarification on your shop before your start date.

Ask Questions Early

If you have any questions about any of the information in the shop instructions, shop survey form, additional instructions, or emails, contact the shop scheduler immediately. The earlier you ask questions the better since schedulers are not available 24/7 and may not be available if you have a question during the shop.

The best way to contact a shop scheduler is usually via email, although some also give phone and text contact info, and some websites allow you to submit a message directly to the scheduler from the shop details page. However you choose to contact the scheduler, try to include all your questions in one conversation or email, and be prepared to wait up to 48 hours for a reply (although some schedulers respond much faster, some are not very responsive at all). If you haven't heard back from the scheduler in 48 hours, reach out again using a different contact method if possible. If you've contacted the scheduler several times with no response, or your shop is to be completed in the next 24 hours, go to the company's website to find their main phone number. The receptionist should be able to connect you with someone that can help.

If you've tried all of this with no luck and you are unsure of how to proceed with the shop, DO NOT complete the shop. One mistake may mean you don't get paid, and it's doubtful they will care that you made attempts to contact someone prior to the shop. If you can't cancel the shop directly from the shop details page, then send the scheduler an email stating that you've made several attempts to contact them with questions but haven't received a response, so you will not be able to complete the shop until someone contacts you for clarification. You may also want to call and leave a voicemail with the scheduler/company. This should be a very rare situation - in over 15 years of mystery shopping I can only recall one scheduler who would not respond to questions at all.

The Day Of Your Shop

Double-Check Shop Details

The day of your shop date (or day before if you prefer or have an early morning shop), log back into the company's website and double check all your shop details - dates, times, address, business name, etc.

Re-Read Everything

From the shop details page, use the links to re-read everything - the shop instructions, shop survey form, and additional instructions. If it's been several days since you first read everything, you may be surprised at what new pieces of info you pick up. Also, if the shop survey form wasn't available to be viewed when you were first assigned the shop, it should definitely be within 24 hours of the shop's start date. Read the survey form thoroughly, especially if this is your first time seeing it.

Download/Print Documents

Now's a good time to download the shop documents to your device or print them out so you can easily review them just before or after the shop. Try not to take shop documents into the shop location if possible. Keep them in your vehicle or bag if you use public transportation. DO NOT pull them out in front of anyone during your shop for any reason - this is why it is so important to review these documents ahead of time. Occasionally a company will allow you to review documents or take notes in the location bathroom or fitting room - this will be noted in the shop's instructions.

Make a Game Plan

Now that all the shop info is fresh on your mind it's time to make your shop game plan. To do this, try to think of completing this shop from beginning to end, from the moment you leave home or work to finishing up and submitting the report. Use your maps app to determine estimated travel times so you can be sure to leave with plenty of time to arrive at the shop location during the assigned time range.

Using the shop instructions, make a list of all required steps of the shop. Try to imagine yourself entering the location and going through each of these steps. Envision yourself interacting with staff, asking them questions, and providing convincing answers. Some shops will give you specific statements or questions to say to staff, while others will allow you to choose a question that best fits your situation. In either case, you need to be familiar enough with what you plan to say for it to be natural and effortless, not forced and rehearsed. Walk through checking out and making a payment in your mind...do you have the required form of payment (some shops require cash or card), did you purchase the correct item(s), is your purchase within the shop's reimbursement amount?

After leaving the shop location, it's best to go to a nearby location to make notes while they're fresh on your mind. If you're completing a shop via an app, you may be able to go ahead and submit the shop right from your mobile device! If not, make relevant notes on the printed shop survey form or in your device's note-taking app, then decide where you will go to actually submit the report. You may need to wait until you get home that evening but as long as you are within the shop's submission deadline that should be fine. Always plan to submit the shop the same day you completed it if possible, even if the submission deadline allows for longer. The longer you take to submit the shop, the more details you will likely forget, and the less accurate your shop survey report will be.

As an example, let's consider a shop at a popular women's clothing store. The shop requires several different interactions, using the fitting room, and a purchase. The shop date/time is 7/26/2022 from 11:30 am to 5 pm. Here's my game plan for completing this shop:

1. Since my work is close to the shop location, and my scheduled lunch break is from 1 pm to 2

pm, I plan to complete this shop during my lunch break.

2. I enter the shop's address into Google Maps and get directions there from my work address. The shop will take 7 minutes to drive to from my work, so if I leave work right at 1 pm, I should be there by 1:10 pm. Also, this means I must leave the shop location by 1:50 pm to arrive back to work on time by 2 pm.

3. Based on the required tasks - question interactions with two different employees, fitting room interaction, and purchase interaction, I estimate this shop will require 30-40 minutes. This should also give me time to deal with anything unusual that comes up.

4. I note the exact time I enter the shop location.

5. The shop instructions require me to ask one employee a question about the store's new rewards program. The specific questions is "What is different about the new rewards program?" I memorize this question and plan to ask the first employee I encounter in the store.

6. The shop instructions state that I can ask a second employee any product-related question I like. Since this store sells women's shoes, I plan to find a pair of shoes and ask if they come in a different color. If there is no employee present in the shoe section, I will carry the shoes with me until I encounter an employee to ask.

7. Only one employee working during my shop? No problem. I'll ask the same employee both questions and describe what happened in my shop survey report.

8. While browsing during these first two employee interactions, I will pick up a few clothing items to take into the fitting room. Since my time is limited I won't actually try the items on, so it doesn't really matter if they are my exact size or even something I would really wear. If you have more time to do your shop, feel free to browse for items you really like and may purchase.

9. I will approach the fitting room attendant with my items and complete the fitting room portion of the shop.

10. While in the fitting room, the shop instructions ask me to time how long it takes for the fitting room attendant to check back on me. If they have not checked back within 5 minutes, I can exit the fitting room without this timing and will indicate this on my report. I'll use the timer on my phone's clock app to make this timing. I just turn the timer on as soon as I enter the fitting room and stop it as soon as the attendant checks on me. Then I'll take a screenshot of the end time so I don't have to remember the exact number. It's easy to just refer back to a photo while filling out your report! ***

11. While I'm waiting in the fitting room, I make some notes on my phone's note-taking app about the names and descriptions of the employees I've already interacted with, their answers to my questions, and the store's overall appearance. Turn the sound off on your device so the employees can't hear you typing! Taking written notes is fine too, but some places don't allow bags in fitting rooms, so plan accordingly.

12. After exiting the fitting room, it's time to make my purchase. According to the shop details and instructions, this shop's reimbursement limit is $10, and I can purchase any item in the store I want. Since I'm a jewelry lover, I browse through their costume jewelry section and pick up an item or two that I like. I like getting everything for free, so I make sure my items won't total to more than $10, including tax. Where I live, the sales tax rate is 6.75%, so my items can't be more than $9.36 before tax. This will vary depending on the sales tax rate where you live.

13. After exiting the store and noting the exact time, I get in my car and drive back to work. With just a few minutes to spare before 2 pm, I make some final notes on my phone's note-taking app about the last part of the shop and snap a photo of my receipt.

14. After work, I will head home and immediately turn in my shop survey report using my laptop.

The company allows me up to 24 hours after the shop ends to submit the report, but since I'm entering it as soon as possible I actually remembered some details that I forgot to include in my notes.

15. After submitting the report, I keep an eye on my email and phone for messages from the shop's editor (the person who reviews the shop before submitting it to the end client). I respond to any questions ASAP but definitely within the time range for answering editor questions as provided in the company's ICA or shop instructions.

Feel free to format your game plan in a more visual way, such as a flow chart or graph, if that's more appealing to you. Once you've got your game plan written out, read it top to bottom several times, making edits and additions during each reading. I suggest saving your game plan to your mobile device so you can make edits as you think of them on the go. I like using the Google Docs app for mobile documents.

After completing several shops you will likely not need to write down your game plans anymore, but feel free to do so as long as you need!

*** If this shop had multiple timings, such as how long until first greeted after entering the store, how long for fitting room attendant to check back, and how long was checkout from entering the line to receiving your receipt, then the "lap" feature on your timer can be very useful. Just start the timer when you enter the store, hit "lap" every time you need to start or stop a timing, and then screenshot the laps and total time at the end. Just run a few practice rounds at the house to get used to using this feature and calculating times.

Shoppers vary greatly in how they choose to record timings, and no way is wrong if it gives you an accurate reading. Don't try to count in your head or use 1-Mississippi, 2-Mississippi,...you'll never get it right and if the store looks back at video and notices big timing discrepancies, your shop may be invalidated and you won't be paid.

Chapter 5 Summary

- You will receive an assignment email if one of your mystery shop applications is approved - keep an eye on your spam or junk folder as well!
- As soon as you are assigned to a shop, confirm all of the shop's details including location, date, time, etc.
- Companies that use the Sassie platform may require you to confirm your assigned shop using a link in your assignment email
- Read all shop documents as soon as possible after assignment, including shop instructions, the shop survey form, and any additional instructions provided by the company or scheduler

- If any of the shop details are incorrect or you have questions about any of the shop documents, contact the shop's scheduler immediately! Do not wait until just before the shop's assigned completion date to ask questions since schedulers are not available 24/7
- On the day of (or evening before) your assigned shop completion date, re-read all the shop details and documents
- Download shop documents to your mobile device or print them and keep them hidden in your bag or purse
- Make a game plan of exactly how you intend to complete all required parts of your assigned shop. Write this plan down and review it many times before your shop, including just before entering the shop location

Chapter 6: What to Know: During the Shop

The day has come and you're sitting in your car, staring at the front door of your assigned shop location, wondering if you can really do this. Don't worry...you got this! Take a deep breath and let's head inside!

Know the Plan

Just before you enter the location look over your game plan one last time. Practice your questions and scenario once more, trying to sound as natural as possible, and imagining how you will respond to questions the staff may ask you. The more you have reviewed your plan and practiced your scenario and questions prior to going into your shop the more natural the entire shop will feel, and you will be much less likely to be spotted as a mystery shopper. Since you can't reference your shop instructions or other documents while you are conducting the shop (unless you sneak away to a bathroom or fitting room, which isn't always possible) you'll have to depend on your memory to make sure you complete all the required steps. Practice, practice, practice!

Avoid Distractions

It's easy to become distracted at any point in time but it seems to happen more often when you know you need to be focused and pay attention. Whether the distraction is your phone ringing, a crying child in the store, or just a gorgeous $500 bag that you're not sure you can live without, distractions are rampant while trying to remember all your tasks for a mystery shop. The best piece of advice I can give you for avoiding distractions is turn your phone to silent mode. This is so important that some companies actually require it and if they see you using your phone during the shop on the store surveillance footage your shop will be invalidated and you will not be paid. There's no way you can be browsing Facebook and giving your shop the amount of focus that it requires at the same time. However, sometimes you may run into a distraction you can't completely avoid. At a recent shop I ran into an acquaintance who wanted to stop and talk. In the spirit of being natural and behaving as a normal customer would, I stood there for a few minutes talking, then politely ended the conversation and we went our separate ways. Sometimes you'll be thrown a curveball like this, and even with the best made game plan you can't avoid it, so just go with it! Always be sure to note things like this in your shop survey report. Most companies understand that these types of things are going to happen, especially when a shopper is shopping a location near their own home. However, if you don't report this in your shop survey report and they happen to see something on the surveillance footage, they may feel that you were being dishonest and invalidate your shop. It's always best to be 100% transparent when filling out your shop survey report, especially about any distractions or unusual situations you may have encountered during the shop.

Maintain Anonymity

If there were a ten commandments of mystery shopping I'm sure one of them would be about maintaining anonymity. If you are conducting a covert shop then you should under no circumstances reveal your identity as a mystery shopper, not to employees, managers, customers, or anyone else.

One of the easiest ways for employees to spot you as a mystery shopper is if your behavior is odd or unnatural. This is why it's so important to practice your questions and practice your scenario before going in the store, especially if you will have to portray a person that is different than yourself. For example, during some shops of financial institutions you may have to portray a wealthy investor or someone who owns a high revenue business. You need to be prepared with the answers to common questions that the employees might ask you during the shop, such as your annual income, business income, diversity of investments, etc. Depending on the type of shop there can be any number of questions an employee may ask you. If an employee asks you a simple question that anyone in your position should quickly know the answer to and you hesitate or stammer through your response they may begin to suspect that you are a mystery shopper.

Maintaining anonymity can also be difficult when you are required to take covert photos. It can be really difficult to take a photo without any employees or customers seeing you, especially if the location you are shopping is small or cramped. However, thanks to the explosion of social media, it's really not uncommon for people to take photos of businesses for them to post in online reviews. If you're ever spotted taking a photo you can always try to play it off like you intend to post a photo in a Google or Facebook review. I once did a fast food shop where the restaurant was located inside of a gas station. There was a small hot bar of prepared food that sat right next to the cash register. The shop required that I take a photo of the items on this hot food bar. This was incredibly difficult since the cashier was standing behind the cash register and there was no way for me to take the photo without her seeing, so I told her that I was going to take a photo of the items to send to my husband so he could decide what he wanted me to order for him. She accepted this reason without hesitation, I snapped the photo, and finished up the shop. Sometimes you have to be a little creative and think on your feet in situations like these, but that's part of what makes mystery shopping so fun!

Taking Notes

The ability to get away to a private place to take notes during a shop is often a luxury. Many shoppers depend on bathrooms and fitting rooms for this purpose. However, stores that do not sell clothing items won't have a fitting room and not all locations have public bathrooms. If you find yourself in a situation where you are worried about forgetting required details and there's no private place to get away, I would suggest whipping out your cell phone very quickly and texting yourself a quick note to help you remember. Do not keep your cell phone out the entire time taking constant notes as this will end up being a distraction and actually stop you from collecting all the information that is required for your shop. If you are using the clock app on your cell phone to do timings for the shop then you may want to text yourself a couple of notes whenever you pull your phone out to lap a timing. Don't feel that you need to write a full narrative in these text notes since you definitely won't have time for that. Instead, use abbreviations and shorthand that you understand. You'll be the only one who actually sees these notes, and you'll be writing them out in a more formal manner when filling out the shop survey report.

Chapter 6 Summary

- Know your shop game plan inside and out before you enter the shop location
- Try your best to avoid distractions by putting your mobile device on silent mode
- Not all distractions are avoidable...sometimes you have to just go with it and get the shop back on track as quickly as possible
- NEVER reveal yourself as a mystery shopper during your shop, unless you are doing a revealed shop

- Take notes in the restroom or fitting room if you can. If this is not possible, text yourself quick notes when possible if you're worried about forgetting details.

Chapter 7: What to Know: After the Shop

Immediate Debriefing

You just finished your shop and have all of these details swirling around in your mind. It's time to debrief! The sooner you jot down the notes from your mind the more accurate they , and your shop survey report, will ultimately be. It is extremely convenient to have a printed shop survey form when doing these debriefing notes. However, don't ever just sit in your car in the location's parking lot writing out notes or filling out the shop survey form that you printed. Always drive to a different location where there's no chance that the store employees will see you. If you use public transportation then take advantage of the riding time and jot down all the important details from your shop while on the way to your next destination. Just like any notes you may have taken during the shop, these debriefing notes do not need to be formal or complete.

Mobile shops note: If you happen to be completing a shop through a mobile app then go ahead and fill out the shop survey report in the app instead of doing debriefing notes. Shops that are conducted through mobile apps are typically shorter and require much less narrative than traditional shops. You should have no problem filling out the mobile shop survey report and submitting photos of any receipts or other collateral in the mobile app.

Submitting a Top-Quality Report

Whenever you get back to a desktop or laptop it's time to start filling out your shop survey report. Make sure you submit your shop survey report within the company's submission deadline!

Go ahead and find the shop assignment email in your inbox, click the link to login to the company's shopper website, and open up the shop's survey report. Depending on the platform that the company uses the shop survey report may look very different. Some companies ask all questions on one long page, like Sassie, while others may split the questions up into several sections over several different pages.

Fill out the report with the information you collected during your shop. Use your notes, photos, screenshots of timings, or any other resources available to you to make filling out the report easier. The first thing I like to do after opening up the shop survey report is to submit all photos, receipts, and other collateral required for the shop. Depending on the shop platform you may be asked to submit these items in different ways, but most commonly you will find an upload link in the shop survey report that will allow you to upload the required files. Most companies include a different upload link for each required item. For example, if a shop on the Sassie platform requires a copy of your receipt, three different photos from inside the store, and a photo of the employee's business card, then there will be five different questions with separate upload links for the five different required items. Some other platforms may only have one upload link where they want you to upload all the required items at one time and label them. Regardless of how the company and platform handles uploads, you definitely will not be paid for your shop without including the required collateral. That's why I always do this part first and save the report as a draft so I know that the items are uploaded successfully to the report. There will typically be a link near the bottom of the page that allows you to save the survey report and return to it later.

For most shops, the majority of questions on the shop survey report are going to be True/False or multiple-choice, and fewer will be narrative style. I suggest first going through and answering all of the True/False or multiple-choice questions and saving your report as a draft again. Some platforms may not allow you to answer the report questions out of order and that's okay, but waiting to do the narratives after you have answered all the other questions gives you a better idea of exactly what information the company is looking for in your narrative responses.

Once you have all the True/False and multiple-choice questions answered and saved, it's time to work on your narratives. I would suggest opening a Microsoft Word or Google Docs document to type your narrative responses first and then copy and paste them into the shop survey report. This makes it easier to spell and grammar check your responses. Even though most platforms offer some sort of spell checker for narrative responses, the spell checkers can be a bit outdated and difficult to use.

Find the first question in the shop survey report that requires a narrative response. Copy and paste this question into your document. Now type up a well-written response using correct grammar and full sentences. No abbreviations or shorthand in narratives!

Mystery shopping companies only want information directly related to the questions being asked in the report, so don't feel the need to fill in your narrative responses with extra info just to make your answer longer. If the narrative box is to summarize your answers in one section of the report, then look back at the True/False and multiple-choice questions you already answered in that section and focus your narrative response on those.

Companies also focus on objectiveness and very rarely want your opinion about anything. Just the facts please! So instead of saying that you think an employee had an attitude, you need to be very specific about why you felt that the employee had the attitude. Was it something specific they said that was rude? If so, provide a quote of exactly what was said. Did they act indifferent towards you or roll their eyes at you? Then be sure to state those exact behaviors. The same goes for friendly, helpful employees. Exactly what did they do to be friendly? Did they smile, make eye contact, or offer to assist you? Did they compliment you on pants you were trying on or offer to bring a different size or color? It's important to be specific.

Now that you've finished your first narrative response, copy and paste the second narrative question from the shop survey report into your document and begin working on your response. Repeat this for each narrative question in the shop survey report. When you've finished with all the narrative responses for your report it's time to check your spelling and grammar. This is where the spell check and grammar check features in your word processing software or possibly browser add-ons will come in very handy. Microsoft Word and Google Docs both have built-in spelling and grammar checkers that I would suggest you use. If you prefer to type directly into the shop survey report instead of using a separate document, I would highly suggest installing a browser add-on or extension that helps check your spelling and grammar. Grammarly is one of the biggest players in this field and is available on every major internet browser. I like to use a combination of the spelling and grammar checker that comes with Google docs in addition to the Grammarly add-on to check on my narrative responses.

Once I feel that my narrative response is well written and answers all of the questions required, I copy and paste it into the shop survey report and save the report as a draft. If you type your narrative responses directly into the report, be sure to save the report after each narrative response so you don't lose multiple responses later on if something happens to your internet connection. Know that some narrative text boxes have a limit on how many characters or words can be in your answer. If you exceed this limit (or go below the minimum limit) you will receive an error message when you attempt to save the report as a draft or submit it. In this case you'll need to go back in and edit your narrative response to meet the character or word count requirements.

Now that you've finished all the True/False, multiple-choice, and narrative responses, it's time to submit your shop survey report. Don't worry too much about missing questions since most sites won't allow you to submit a final report if any required questions are not answered. For example, for a Sassie-based company, if you attempt to submit the report before all required questions are answered you will get an error page that tells you how many "Oops" answers you had. There will be a link for you to click back into the shop survey report and review all of the "Oops" questions. Once you have corrected all the "Oops" questions you can scroll down to the bottom of the survey report page and submit again.

If all the required questions are answered and everything looks correct you will receive a shop submission confirmation page. This page will often allow you to download a copy of the shop you submitted. This download will usually be a PDF or some type of image file. I would highly recommend that you always download a copy of your submitted shop survey report when possible. This way, if the company has questions about your shop two or three months from now, you can easily refer back to the copy of your shop survey report that you saved to see what your answers were. If you complete many different mystery shops it is very easy to get details from different places mixed up. Saving copies of all of your shop-related info, such as a copy of your submitted report, photos you submitted, photos of receipts, business cards, or other collateral, in one central place is key to staying organized and being successful as a mystery shopper. I personally use Google Drive for this purpose because it's free to use and I can access it anywhere I have an internet connection, including via an app on my smartphone. Any storage, whether it's cloud storage or just saving it to your hard drive, is acceptable. I have a folder in Google Drive dedicated to mystery shopping and a subfolder for each company I work with, which has been dozens over the years.

Editor Requests

After you submit your shop survey report it will be sent to a shop editor for review. The shop editor goes over each answer in your report to make sure that you followed the shop instructions and met all required guidelines. They will also review the photos and other collateral you uploaded to the report to make sure that they match the assigned location, date, and time. If anything is missing or unclear in your shop the editor will usually email you and ask for clarification. This is why it's very important to keep a close eye on your email inbox for questions or requests from the editor until you receive notification that your report was approved. Some editors may even call you in an attempt to get the information over the phone. I prefer to communicate with editors via email just because there is a written trail where I can prove what information I was asked for and what information I provided.

If an editor contacts you with a question or a request for a missing item, you need to respond to this request ASAP. Some companies do set a deadline of 12 to 24 hours to respond to an editor request, but it's always better to respond as quickly as possible while the information is fresh on your mind. This also gives the editor time to review the new information and include it in your shop survey report before it needs to be sent off to the end client. Keep in mind that some companies may take quite some time to get back with you about questions on your report, which is why it is so important to always save copies of your completed report and any photos or other collateral that you submitted. When an editor asks you a question about a shop that you completed two months ago it can be incredibly difficult to remember exactly what happened. Stay organized and keep copies of everything so you don't end up getting your shop invalidated later on because you forgot something or couldn't answer an editor's question.

Getting Paid

Now that you've completed your shop, submitted a top-notch report, and responded to all editor requests, it's time to get paid! All companies have different pay policies so you'll need to be familiar with each company's individual policy. This may seem overwhelming at first, but after working with the same company for several shops you get the hang of how and how often they pay. It's also important to note that a few companies require shoppers to send in an invoice after completing a shop. They may want an invoice after each shop you complete or a monthly invoice with all shops completed in that month. These companies will explain this process clearly when you are registering with them and also with each shop you are assigned. Most companies do not require shoppers to send in an invoice.

While some mobile shops pay as quickly as 48 hours, it is much more common for your shop to pay at some point in the month following the month you completed the shop. For example, if you complete a shop in the month of April, expect to get paid sometime in May. This payment will include any authorized reimbursement for purchases and bonus pay.

How you will receive your payment will depend on what options you selected when you registered with the company. Most companies these days prefer PayPal, direct deposit, or some similar digital payment service, but there are still some out there that pay via paper check in the mail. Review the company's pay policy to get an idea of when you should be expecting your payment. Then keep an eye out in your PayPal or bank account (or mailbox) around this date. If several days to a week has gone by past the date that you expected payment and you still haven't received anything, reach out to the company. Some of these companies process literally thousands of shop payments each payroll and sometimes things get lost in the shuffle. The company can't know that you were not paid unless you let them know so it's important to be prompt and courteous with any missing payment requests

Once you have received your payment, double check it against the shop pay, reimbursement, and bonus pay you expected to receive for the shop. If the payment you received is not what you expected then reach out to the company to find out what happened.

It's important to keep good records of the shops you complete and payments you receive so you can be sure you've received everything to which you are entitled.

See the last chapter of this book on Record-Keeping for more information.

Chapter 7 Summary

- As soon as you exit the shop location, write shorthand, abbreviated debriefing notes of all the important details of the shop
- Write debriefing notes as soon as possible after exiting the shop's location so you remember more details
- Mobile apps shops can possibly be submitted during debriefing if narratives are not required
- Always try to submit your shop's report on the same day that the shop was completed, but always within the company's submission deadline
- Tackle the shop survey report in an organized, methodical fashion
- Attach collateral to the shop survey report first
- Type narrative responses out in a separate word document when possible to make spelling and grammar checking easier, then copy and paste to the shop survey report fields
- Focus your narrative responses on just the questions asked in the shop survey report
- Be specific about statements or actions taken by employees
- Keep your opinions to yourself in narrative responses - just the facts please!

- Monitor your email and respond to editor requests for clarification or more information as soon as possible
- Know the company's pay policy and monitor your accounts for the shop's payment
- Compare the shop payment received to the amount you expected...report any discrepancies to the company quickly

Chapter 8: Record-Keeping

So you've put in the work and have finally been paid for your first shop. Congratulations! You may be tempted to take your new earnings and go get a massage or take the family out for a nice dinner. But wait...there may be a few things you want to think about first. Since virtually all mystery shopping work is done as an independent contractor you can now consider yourself a small business owner. As with any business, there are decisions that need to be made and records that need to be kept. Don't be overwhelmed by the idea of maintaining books for a business...technology today makes it very easy to keep track of everything you need to make record-keeping and tax time a breeze.

Business Setup

The first thing you need to do is decide on a name and structure for your business. While these decisions can go beyond the scope of this book depending on how complicated your personal and tax situation is, most mystery shoppers opt to structure their business as a sole proprietorship under their own personal name. This is exactly what I did for many years. However, depending on your situation, you might find it more appropriate to structure your business as a partnership, LLC, or incorporation. If you choose one of these structures you will likely want to name your business something other than your personal name.

Regardless of what business structure you decide to use you'll need to check with your city, county, and state for laws and rules on how to register your business. Some states do not require sole proprietorships to be registered while others do. Using an LLC or incorporation structure can lead to some pretty complicated paperwork that may require the assistance of an attorney or accountant. All businesses, regardless of structure, or required to be registered in the county where I live but my state does not require sole proprietorships or general partnerships to be registered with the Secretary of State. The rules in your area will likely vary greatly so take advantage of all the information out there on the web and make sure you are setting your business up legally. Failing to register your business using the appropriate channels could lead to some pretty hefty fines or legal trouble.

The business structure you decide to use will also affect how you will fill out taxes for the income you earn mystery shopping. See the section later on on tax implications for more information.

Personal Shop Log

Now that you've got your business named, structured, and registered, it's time to actually start keeping up with the shops you complete and payments you receive. How you do this is completely up to you. Some people build elaborate spreadsheets to track all this information, some people use a CPA or bookkeeper, and some people still write it all down using pen and paper. It's all about what's the most comfortable for you.

Since I have received a confirmation email for every mystery shop I've ever done I decided to take advantage of this and use my emails label feature to track my assigned shops. Whenever I receive an email related to a shop assignment I attached a label to it named "MS Assignments", which automatically places the email in a folder of this same name. This allows me to easily look into the folder and see all the mystery shops that were assigned to me along with any modification or cancellation emails I may have received. Since most confirmation emails also include payment information for the shop, I can also easily see how much I was supposed to be paid when checking this against the funds I actually received.

To check payments, I simply open my "MS Assignments" folder in my email in one browser tab and open my bank account activity or PayPal account activity in another tab. Then I can easily flip back and forth between the two comparing the payments I received in my accounts to the expected payment from my confirmation emails. If I don't see a payment that I should have received I can quickly open another browser tab to go to that company site, double check their pay policy, and contact them if necessary. I try to go through the email folder every 2 to 3 months to verify I have received the payments that I had expected.

Again, many people choose to use accounting software for small businesses or customize spreadsheets to keep up with assigned shops, and these methods work very well. You can find many spreadsheet templates on the internet made specifically for mystery shoppers. However, I like to keep things as simple as possible so taking the time to enter all my assigned shop information into a software program or spreadsheet is unappealing to me. Paperwork is something you won't get paid for as a mystery shopper so try to keep the time you spend on it to a minimum.

Tracking Mileage & Expenses

It's very important to track your mileage and expenses related to your mystery shopping business. Since your business operates out of your home address, you will be able to claim miles driven from your home to the shop's location and back as business miles. I like to use Google Maps to calculate my mileage, but it's perfectly fine to write it in a paper mileage log if you prefer. If you do not drive but instead take public transportation to and from shops, you will be able to claim these transportation expenses as a business deduction on your federal income taxes, so keep copies of all statements and receipts for transportation, parking, tolls, and any other travel-related costs.

While mileage or transportation costs will likely be your highest expense in mystery shopping, there are other expenses you will want to track as well, including but not limited to:

- Home office expenses
- Supplies

- Business use of your mobile device and service plan
- Business use of your home internet connection
- Unreimbursed shop expenses
- Fees or dues paid to professional organizations (such as the MSPA)
- Overnight travel expenses

You may have more or less types of expenses to track for your business, depending on the types of shops you complete. Always consult with a financial professional, such as a certified accountant, if you are unsure about what you need to track.

Tax Decisions

Even though a mystery shopping company will not issue you a 1099 for mystery shopping income unless you make $600 or more with them in one year, this doesn't mean the IRS doesn't want you to report your mystery shopping income, no matter how small. It's very important to understand how to file taxes for the business structure you choose. Taxes for a sole proprietorship or a general partnership that qualifies as a joint venture for federal tax purposes are by far the easiest types of business taxes to complete. However, depending on your personal situation, one of these business structures may not be appropriate and you may need to learn more about filing taxes for a more complicated business structure such as an LLC or incorporation. In this case I would highly suggest speaking with an accountant or attorney who is well-versed in business taxes so they can guide you on exactly what you need to be keeping up with during the year. To keep things simple we are going to focus on taxes for a mystery shopping business structure as a sole proprietorship.

You're going to need to keep up with some pretty basic information over the year in order to do your business taxes. You'll need your total shop pay received, bonus pay received, reimbursements received, total shop expenses (broken down into the categories mentioned in the last section), and square footage of your home office if applicable. I use the simple method of calculating my home office deduction by just entering the square footage of my home office space into my tax preparation software. This might not always lead to the biggest deduction but it's a lot less work than the second method which requires much more detailed information about the home office and expenses. Both ways are fine to use and if you're willing to put in the extra effort on the possibility of a larger deduction then feel free to go with the second method.

As a sole proprietor you will file a minimum of a Schedule C and Schedule SE in addition to your form 1040, and any other forms or schedules that may be required depending on your tax situation. Any professional tax preparer should be well aware of what forms to file for a sole proprietorship. Many of the online tax preparation software also includes features that can do business taxes for a sole proprietorship, however, most do not include this in their free version. I use Credit Karma tax preparation software online to complete my personal and business taxes since they are one of the few that allow sole proprietors and partnerships that qualify as a joint venture to file business taxes for free. If you do not feel comfortable filing your own business taxes using online software, I strongly suggest that you consult with a professional tax preparer for assistance with filing your business' taxes.

Chapter 8 Summary

- Mystery shoppers own their own businesses
- Decide on a business structure and register your business with your city, county, and state, as applicable
- Keep a personal shop log of all the shops you've completed and the expected pay for each shop
- Compare your expected payments for shops to the actual amounts you receive and resolve any discrepancies
- Track all expenses related to your mystery shopping business for tax purposes
- Consult a tax professional or accountant for more help on structuring your business and tracking income and expenses

Conclusion/Action Plan

You should now have all the information you need to get started in the mystery shopping business...a business of your very own! While this book is by no means exhaustive in terms of search methods, companies, apps, or advice, it should guide the new shopper to plenty of opportunities and ideas. The mystery shopping industry is constantly changing and evolving, so new ways to find and complete shops could pop up anyday!

If you decide you want to pursue mystery shopping then you can take pride in knowing that your work will actually help shape the future for every business that you shop. Your observations can get an employee a raise or promotion or spark a complete retraining session for a location's entire staff. It goes so much further than just a free meal or oil change!

While this is important work, it's also important to have fun with the shops and all the extra cash in your pocket, meals in your stomach, and new clothes in your closet! Good luck with your new mystery shopping business!

Action Plan:

- Research laws about setting up a business in your city, county, and state
- Decide on a business structure and register your business as required

- Create a mystery shopping email address
- Create an autofill profile in your browser just for mystery shopping
- Register with shop aggregators - Jobslinger and MS Job Board
- Use the aggregators to find companies that offer shops in your area
- Register with each company that offers shops in your area and search their job boards
- Apply for shops you are interested in and monitor your email for assignment emails
- Repeat these steps with mobile aggregator apps, forums, and social media groups to find more companies
- Review all shop documents and details thoroughly as soon as you are assigned, several times before your shop date, and also just before you conduct the shop
- Make a shop game plan from the shop instructions and know it by heart!
- Debrief important shop information as soon as you leave the shop location
- Submit all parts of the shop survey report as soon as possible while details are fresh on your mind
- Respond to editor requests promptly
- Make sure the payment you receive is correct
- Keep a personal shop log with income and expenses for tax purposes
- Have fun!!!

About the Expert

Mystery shopping since the early 2000's, Penny Hodgin has seen and adapted to many changes in the mystery shopping industry. What began as a teenager's side hustle to earn some extra cash and free meals has evolved into a passion for helping businesses treat their customers and employees with the respect they deserve by providing honest observations and factual reports. Hodgin has shopped professionally in various industries including retail, financial, entertainment, real estate, food service, and more...and has truly enjoyed the experience gained from each and every shop!

Hodgin lives on the East US Coast with her husband, two children, and grandmother. She graduated with a Bachelor's in Human Services in 2010 and has worked full-time in the mental health and education fields. She plans to retire to the beach as soon as possible!

HowExpert publishes quick 'how to' guides on all topics from A to Z by everyday experts. Visit HowExpert.com to learn more.

Recommended Resources

- HowExpert.com – Quick 'How To' Guides on All Topics by Everyday Experts.
- HowExpert.com/books – HowExpert Books
- HowExpert.com/products – HowExpert Products
- HowExpert.com/courses – HowExpert Courses
- HowExpert.com/clothing – HowExpert Clothing
- HowExpert.com/membership – Learn All Topics from A to Z by Real Experts.
- HowExpert.com/affiliates – HowExpert Affiliate Program
- HowExpert.com/jobs – HowExpert Jobs
- HowExpert.com/writers – Write About Your #1 Passion/Knowledge/Expertise.
- YouTube.com/HowExpert – Subscribe to HowExpert YouTube.
- Instagram.com/HowExpert – Follow HowExpert on Instagram.
- Facebook.com/HowExpert – Follow HowExpert on Facebook.

Made in United States
Orlando, FL
05 December 2021

11171599R00057